The Camping Cookbook

SARA
MUTANDE

ANDREA
LO VETERE

Beatnik

Beatnik

P O Box 8276, Symonds Street,
Auckland 1150, New Zealand

First published in 2019 by
Beatnik Publishing

Illustration, Design and
Typesetting: ©Sara Mutande
and Andrea Lo Vetere 2019

ISBN 978-0-9951180-0-3

Printed and bound in China using
Forest Stewardship Council™
(FSC™)–certified paper and other
controlled material.

The Camping Cookbook

SARA
MUTANDE

ANDREA
LO VETERE

Beatnik

Contents

4. EXAMPLES

5. INDEX

6. NOTES

Introduction

There's so much to love about camping: getting back to nature, forgetting about all the stresses of urban life, and not having to think about how your hair looks today. And yet the simple pleasures of being out in the wild usually means eating as if centuries of culinary refinement never happened. Well, not anymore.

This collection of field-tested recipes turns the whole idea of roughing it on its head. We've made a virtue out of simplicity by returning to the enduring fundamentals of traditional cooking. By using the easy-to-find ingredients common to the world's most popular dishes, you'll be able to make the best out of less.

We've put the emphasis on quick cooking times, we've avoided using perishable and bulky goods, and we've used the same pots, pans and utensils you already take on a trip, i.e.: hardly any.

We're also sharing our many hard-won hacks, that'll save you time and effort in every aspect of camp cooking, from planning ahead to washing up afterwards.

It doesn't matter if you're cooking on a pocket stove on some remote beach, relaxing in a campervan, or hanging around a bonfire with friends – the Camping Cookbook will inspire you with delicious risottos, glorious pastas, tasty snacks and desserts, and maybe even the odd pizza. Yes, pizza.

Enjoy.

Sara & Andrea

Hi, I'm Sara. I grew up between the pots, pans and plants in my family home, which is one of the most awarded country lodges in Extremadura, Spain. I divide my professional life between being a chef and an illustrator.

And I'm Andrea, from Sicily. I'm known among my friends as the Italiban because of my extreme fundamentalism regarding traditional Italian recipes. When I'm not cooking or camping I work as a graphic designer.

When we moved to New Zealand a few years ago, we embraced the Kiwi outdoor lifestyle. But as foodies, we resolved never to forgo the pleasures of eating well, even on a five-day hike in the southern fjords, where every kilo in your backpack makes each step feel ten times heavier.

So, during our travels we've perfected the many recipes and hard-won cooking hacks that we share in this book, all of which would have read very strangely without the help of David Bell, who's translated our Spanish and Italian versions of English into something less unintentionally amusing.

1.
Equipment & Supplies

Coco Chanel once said, 'Before you leave the house, look in the mirror and remove one accessory.' We say lose the mirror too.

Before you go camping, think about what's really going to make your trip enjoyable, and reduce things to the essential. By using interchangeable ingredients and multifunctional utensils, you can strike the perfect balance between keeping things simple and still being able to indulge your love of good food.

It doesn't mean doing without, rather it's about getting the most out of what you take. In cooking more simply, you'll rediscover your more inventive, less wasteful self, and that is a wonderfully satisfying experience. And who knows, by decluttering and being more adaptable in our everyday lives, maybe we'd all be better off.

Food Shopping List

Years of trial and error have helped us assemble our list of grab-and-go essentials and all the ingredients that transform the simple into the indulgent. We always check everything off before any trip, not because we get any pleasure from lists (we just want to get out there) but because a few moments of planning always makes things easier in the long run.

STAPLES
Without these, nothing else works.

- Extra-virgin olive oil
- Salt
- Sugar
- Herbs and spices: oregano, pepper, rosemary, smoked paprika are the essentials for savoury dishes. Cinnamon, vanilla, cardamom for sweet ones, and if you find herbs like sage, rosemary or thyme in the wild, pick them up and bring them with you
- Soy sauce
- Dry yeast

FAST CARBS
Fast carbs. Highly nutritious and fast to cook, they are the base ingredient for many of your meals.

- Pasta (avoid slow cooking, thick kinds of pasta)
- Bread: buns and sliced
- Wrapping tortillas
- Couscous
- Quinoa
- Rice (consider fast-cooking rice)
- Breadcrumbs
- High-grade flour
- Chickpea flour

DRY FOOD

Almost zero weight, tasty and makes a great stock when hydrated.

- Mushrooms
- Stock cubes
- Mashed potatoes
- Cheeckpea flour
- Powdered milk
- Coffee
- Nuts and dry fruit
- Sundried tomatoes
- Textured soy (vegetarian long-life substitute for minced meat)
- Biscuits

PRESERVED FOOD

Best made yourselves, at home.

- Olives
- Capers
- Basil pesto

PERISHABLE FOOD

Depending on your refrigeration possibilities.

- Vegetables (prefer fast cooking veggies like leek, mushrooms, courgette, onion, tomato...)
- Fruit (Avocados, bananas, berries, oranges and lemons)
- Cheese (at least a melting cheese for cooking and an aged cheese for taste)
- Eggs
- Milk (long-life, in small bricks)

CANNED FOOD

A compact way to bring key ingredients.

- Chickpeas
- Lentils
- Chopped tomato
- Tuna

Basic Equipment

It doesn't matter whether we're backpacking or pootling around in a flash campervan, we're all guilty of cramming our bags with too much 'stuff'. But remember that part of the joy in going camping is getting away from civilisation, and that less really is more. Our bottom-line list of tools is really all you need:

GAS STOVE

You probably already have one, so there are only two things left to remember: take enough gas bottles for your whole trip, and check they're compatible with your stove before you go.

POTS

You need at least two pots, preferably lightweight aluminium, both with lids. One should be big enough for boiling up bulky veggies, cooking pasta, and making soups. The smaller one is for fiddlier things like sauces. If weight isn't an issue, or you're built like a Bulgarian shot-putter, consider bringing a cast-iron Dutch oven. And a strainer.

FRYING PAN/SKILLET

Again, if weight and space aren't issues, bring one along (you'll definitely need to if you want to make our pizza recipe). But one of your normal pans might do the job. If you're travelling really light, a dedicated camping set will include a suitable shallow-sided pan.

BOWL/TUPPERWARE

'Nestable' Tupperware-style plastic bowls keep food fresh, and take up less and less space as you use up your supplies. You want good strong seals and reasonably sturdy plastic, so don't waste money on cheap brands that might split and spill.

CUTLERY

Everyone should have 1 plate, 1 knife, 1 fork, and 1 spoon. Metal plates and cutlery aren't much heavier than plastic, they won't snap, and they last longer. Plus, a long-handled wooden spoon will serve many purposes.

CUPS

Preferably stackable and plastic. With cups, there's no need for glasses, as you can only drink out of one thing at a time. (**Tip:** A cup is also the basic measurement unit for most of our recipes.)

CHOPPING BOARD

An iPad-sized plastic (or preferably wooden) board is almost weightless and packs away easily. But you'll be astonished by the alternative uses you'll find for it.

KNIFE

Entire sections of camping stores are devoted to outdoorsy blades, but our rule is if you have a knife you can cut up a pumpkin with, that's the only one you need. Pay more for a quality , stiff-bladed, medium-sized knife and it will last forever.

ZIP-TOP BAGS

These are the Swiss army knives of storage. We use them for everything, from storing food to freezing water, to breadcrumbing, and at a pinch, to isolate stinky socks. It's worth spending a couple of dollars more for good, strong bags, trust us.

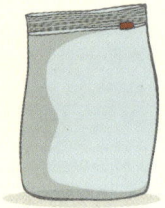

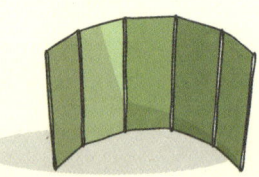

WINDSHIELD

If you have space in your pack, a dedicated windshield makes your stove work more efficiently and safely, and is much easier than laboriously constructing a wall of stones and lumps of wood.

CAN OPENER

Cans are very easy to hack into with a good, wickedly sharp, pointed knife. Unfortunately, so are your fingers. Please, buy a simple lightweight can opener, or use the one on your Swiss army knife or Leatherman.

GRATER

Because a pasta without cheese is like a day without sunshine.

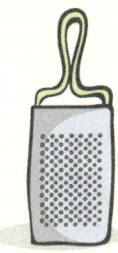

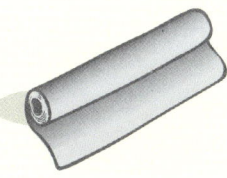

ALUMINIUM FOIL

Wrapping uneaten food? A mouldable cooking pot? Our most useful foil hack is that it turns a pan into an oven, and an oven into an even better oven.

WASHING TOOLS

Eco-friendly soap and a heavy-duty sponge are the bare minimum. If you have space, a plastic washing-up bowl or handled tub or bucket can be a lifesaver. If you're short on space, your biggest cooking pot makes a perfectly adequate washing-up bowl.

Need a Coffee?

INSTANT COFFEE

- PRACTICALITY: ★★★
- TASTE: ★
- IDEAL FOR: a fast coffee hit, especially if you're in a big group. Tell yourself you're in a rush, and that with sugar and milk, it'll do as your breakfast.

Coffee isn't an outdoor luxury, it's a fundamental necessity.

Coffee not only wakes you up, it also fills you up. It smells great, it's sociable, it's warming, and although instant coffee has its place, there's an elemental ritual in making it properly. Above all coffee is cool, especially when it is piping hot. Which is why you always see cowboys drinking coffee in the movies.

And, for balance, there's tea, which we reserve for special moments requiring a more meditative, relaxed and civilised mindset. Or if there are any Brits in our party.

PLUNGER COFFEE

- PRACTICALITY: ★★
- TASTE: ★★
- IDEAL FOR: any time you
  need a coffee. Just boil water
  and infuse the coffee. Repeat
  the process adding some
  more coffee if necessary.

MOKA

- PRACTICALITY: ★
- TASTE: ★★★
- IDEAL FOR: when you
  need a treat. The process is
  marginally slower, but the
  result turns camping into
  glamping.

Storage

On one hand, storage means preserving food longer and reducing cross-contamination of smells and flavours. On the other, it means saving on space and weight, and being able to find ingredients more easily. These are our thoughts on both:

BOXES

In a car? Banana boxes are great. Being shallow, they make it easier to get at what's inside them. Pack in boxes dedicated to similar stuff.

We recommend:
- 1 box for food staples
- 1 for non-perishable food
- 1 for long-life fruit and veggies
- 1 box (or a washing tub) for your cooking gear

SOFT PLASTIC BOTTLES

Glass breaks, so decant oil, vinegar, wine, honey, syrups etc. into soft bottles with airtight seals. When empty, squeeze out the air, store, and reuse later.

ZIP-TOP BAGS

Incredibly space and weight efficient. More importantly, they keep food fresher for longer, they're perfect for storing dried stuff, and they can be used to freeze liquids and wet food.

Also, they have many other practical uses, like breadcrumbing and mixing ingredients (or isolating smelly socks!). Heavier-duty bags with good seals are best, and/or double-bag if you're worried about leaks. Remember to label contents clearly- you don't want to mix sugar with salt!

Tip: See next page for great short-term ice-pack ideas.

Refrigeration

If you're travelling in a half-decent campervan, refrigeration isn't a worry. Otherwise, keeping things cold is a camping storage challenge. A chilly bin is your best friend, but they can be bulky. Fortunately, if you need to keep things light, soft-sided thermal bags come in a variety of shapes and sizes. Whatever kind of cooler you choose to bring, here are our coolest cooling tips.

ICE PACKS

They're reusable, and some are flexible – great for filling up spaces in your chilly bin. Or make your own ice packs by freezing zip-top bags full of wet food and liquids.

Ditto freezing bottles of drinking water or fruit juices. They'll keep your bin cool for a couple of days, and once they've melted you've got fresh, clean drinks.

Tip: A couple of tsp of salt added to water make it freeze faster and stay colder for longer. When the water melts, use it to cook pasta or rice.

ORDER

Schooldays fact reminder: cold air sinks. So raw meat, dairy, frozen food etc. should go to the bottom of your chilly bin where they will stay colder for longer. Fruit and vegetables will be OK on top. Also, remember that every time you open a chilly bin it loses precious cold air, so if you're taking two coolers, set one aside for drinks (you'll be opening that one most).

CLEANING

A cheap sponge on the bottom of your cooler absorbs leaks, keeping things dry and cleaner for longer.

2.
Home
Preparing

Let's come clean: we pre-prepare a lot of food before we go camping. Is that cheating? Yes and no.

Yes because it's a sneaky way of achieving restaurant-quality food, even when the nearest restaurant is two days' walk away. But no, because there's a delicious anticipation in knowing that what we're making at home is going to be especially tasty when we finally get to eat it. We love the satisfaction of delayed gratification. Even more selfishly, all the work done at home (usually when we're cooking anyway) gives us more free time when we're on holiday.

Advance prep also means missing out on soiling your body with processed, pre-acidulated, pre-basted, pre-deseeded, pre-emulsified, pre-saturated junk food.

So here are our tips for doing as much as you can in advance. You will be amazed at what a difference a few pre-prepared sauces and handmade preserves will make to the enjoyment of your trip.

Preserving Food

Many foodstuffs exposed to a wet and warm environment quickly spoil, which is wasteful, and worse, it can result in embarrassing dashes to the toilet. Refrigeration is the modern answer, but using salt, vinegar, sugar, and drying food are all traditional and reliable ways of preserving food. A hidden bonus of these classical cooking methods is that they often make things tastier and more interesting. Here are a few basic, common-sense hacks to preserve your homemade deliciousness for when you're out and about on camp.

DEHYDRATED FOOD

This is the best option for camping because dried food lasts much longer, weighs far less, and yet still retains most of its nutritional goodness. Plus, when you rehydrate it, any excess water instantly makes a great stock.

Fancy drying machines are the best way to dehydrate food, but your kitchen oven works just as well. The key thing is to cut your food into uniformly sized small cubes or thin slices.

Then arrange everything in an even layer on a tray and gently heat it at 100°C, evaporating the water from the food without really cooking it. Depending on what you're baking, an hour will be long enough. When done, take the food out, flip the lot, and repeat the process so that everything is dried all the way through.

Ideal for: Virtually any fruits and veggies, as well as most lean boned meats.

IN OLIVE OIL

In essence, all this requires is submerging your food entirely in extra-virgin olive oil. Refrigerated, it will last several weeks, but only a couple of days once out. You can try vacuum-sealing your pack (see right). When you retrieve the food, use the excess olive oil for cooking.

Saving dry food in oil releases all its flavour into the oil, and vice versa. For sundried tomatoes it's a must, but try it with dried mushrooms and chillies.

Ideal for: Pestos, dry food...

IN SALT

Salt-preserved food won't taste salty, because you wash or brush the salt off before eating. Cut the food uniformly into small pieces or slices. All surfaces must be covered with salt, so first line the bottom of the container (Tupperware is ideal) with salt. Alternate layers of food and salt with salt the last layer.

Ideal for: Capers, small cut veggies...

VACUUM PACKING

This means forcing all the air out of the glass jar you'll be keeping the food in.

Shop-bought jars of jams or pasta sauces are ideal- their lids incorporate simple built in pop-up safety features.

Both jar and lid should be sterilised by boiling them in water for at least 10 mins. Then pour your cooked homemade sauce, pesto etc., into the jar, leaving 1 cm empty at the top. Close the lid very tightly and put it into a pot of cold water, covering it completely. Bring the water to the boil, and keep it boiling for at least 15 min. This will force any air out of the jar. Leave the jar to cool down in the same water. If you've done everything properly, the pop-up lid won't move when pressed.

Tip: Wrapping the jars in clean cloths will stop them cracking against each other while they're boiling.

Ideal for: Sauces, pestos, marmalade, liquid in general...

Soffritto in Salt

This mix of finely cut aromatic vegetables is the base for many classic Mediterranean dishes. Preparing a jar of raw soffritto in salt ahead of time is easy and will save you the effort of carting bulky veggies around. At camp, just stir-fry one tbsp of soffritto in extra-virgin olive oil to start your dish. If you can't make a preserved soffritto in advance, you can substitute it with fresh onion, celery and carrot, finely cut. Remember, when you use Soffritto in Salt in other recipes, you won't need to add any salt for seasoning, as this mix already has enough.

INGREDIENTS

- 200g onion
- 100g celery
- 100g carrot
- 100g coarse salt

PREPARATION

1. Peel the onion, wash the carrot and the celery and dry them carefully.

2. Cut all the vegetables in chunks, put them in a blender and roughly blitz them.

3. Put the mixture in a bowl, add the salt and mix well with a spoon.

4. Put the mixture into a glass jar, close well and store the jar in a dry and cool place. It will last 2 months in the fridge and a few days out of the fridge, enough for your camping trip.

Assorted Zip-top Bags

Zip-top bags prefilled with different mixtures help make camp cooking a doddle. These are our two unmissable bags. See also our recipes for Blueberry Cornmeal Pancakes and Breakfast Porridge.

BREADCRUMB BAG

- Breadcrumbs
- Salt
- Spices: oregano, ground pepper

You'll need a reasonably big zip-top, and only half fill it (the rest of the space is for whatever you're breadcrumbing). Seal it up, then thoroughly mix all the ingredients by shaking the bag vigorously, and that's it, you're ready to pack.

At the camp, just coat the food you want to breadcrumb, in either beaten eggs or hydrated chia seeds (see p. 70), put it into the bag, zip it back up, then shake gently until all the food is thoroughly covered in the breadcrumbs.

HOT CHOCOLATE BAG

- 4 tbsp unsweetened cocoa
- 4 tbsp white sugar
- 4 tbsp dry milk powder
- 2 tbsp cornstarch
- 2 tbsp chocolate chips

Thoroughly mix all the ingredients in a zip-top bag, and pack it. Done. At camp, for each cup of hot chocolate, put 4 tbsp of the mixture in a pot. Add 1/4 cup of water per serving and stir well until you have a thick texture with no lumps. Over a low flame, slowly add the rest of the water. Keep mixing until boiling, and serve hot.

Tip: Spice up your chocolate bag adding either a pinch of salt or chilli, or orange zest.

Pesto Genovese

You'll find dozens of basil pesto brands at the supermarket, but none will taste as good as your homemade version. On camp you can use it to simply season your vegetables, or just dollop your raw pesto into freshly cooked pasta: you'll have a fantastic meal ready in a few minutes. The secret for a long-life sauce is vacuum-sealing it in its jar and keeping it completely covered in olive oil at all times.

INGREDIENTS

- 1 cup fresh basil leaves
- 1/4 cup extra-virgin olive oil
- 1/2 cup finely grated Parmesan cheese
- 1 tbsp pine nuts
- 1/2 garlic clove

PREPARATION

1. Put the basil, garlic and pine nuts in a food blender and mix at low speed, just long enough to roughly smash everything up.

2. Add the olive oil little by little while mixing, and keep mixing until you get a creamy sauce.

3. Add the grated Parmesan cheese and mix well with a spoon.

4. Put the pesto in a small glass jar and vacuum-seal it following the instructions on page 24.

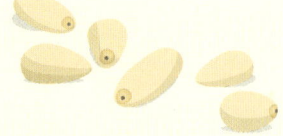

Sundried Tomato Pesto

Spread this Sicilian sauce on a piece of bread for a tasty dip, or just drop it as it is onto your al dente pasta for a delicious, easy-to-make main. Remember to keep the sauce submerged in extra-virgin olive oil to preserve it for longer.

INGREDIENTS

- 1 cup sundried tomatoes
- 1 cup fresh mint
- 1/2 garlic clove
- 1/4 cup extra-virgin olive oil
- 1/2 cup finely grated Parmesan cheese
- 1 tbsp capers
- 2 tbsp walnuts

PREPARATION

1. Put the sundried tomatoes, mint, and garlic in a food blender and mix until you get a grainy paste.

2. Add the olive oil little by little while mixing, and keep going until you get a creamy sauce.

3. Smash the walnuts roughly, then add them to the mix, together with the grated Parmesan. Mix well with a spoon.

4. Put the pesto in a small glass jar and vacuum-seal it following the instructions on page 24.

Tuna in Olive Oil

Preserved tuna is a super versatile ingredient. You can use it to enrich a salad, a sandwich (p. 61) or as a main ingredient for a pasta (p. 41). There are many brands of preserved tuna in the supermarket, but it is much tastier, healthier and cheaper if you start from fresh and do it at home.

INGREDIENTS

- Fresh tuna fillets
  (min 300g)
- 3 cloves of garlic
- 1 tbsp whole pepper
- 3 bay leaves
- 1 tbsp salt
- Extra-virgin olive oil
  (enough to fill your jar)

PREPARATION

1. Remove any bones and dark parts from your fillets of tuna.

2. Boil a pot of water with salt and turn off the stove.

3. Lower the prepared tuna fillets in the just-boiled water and put the lid on the pot. Leave the tuna gently cooking in the cooling heat of the water for at least 30 min.

4. When cool, remove the fillets from the water, handling them carefully, trying not to break up the flesh into chunks. Use a kitchen paper towel to dry the fillets completely.

5. Finally put the fillets in a sterilised glass jar. Add garlic, bay leaves and pepper, and fill up the jar with olive oil until all the tuna flesh is completely covered.

6. Boil the jar in a bain-marie to preserve it (see how to vacuum-seal on page 24).

Homemade Stock

It's no secret that stock is the key of many successful dishes. There's no shortage of commercial stocks at the supermarket, but none will give your dishes half of the taste you'll achieve with this recipe. You can craft your stock with pretty much anything you like- we've used a mix of meat and vegetables – but leave out the meat if you prefer a vegetarian version. A teaspoon of our dried stock dissolved in a pot of boiling water will supercharge the flavour of any dish.

INGREDIENTS

- 300g low-fat meat (beef or chicken thigh)
- 600g vegetables (whatever you fancy most, but carrots, celery, onions, leeks, and mushrooms are our favourites)
- 3 tbsp extra-virgin olive oil
- 2 tbsp white wine
- 300g sea salt (yes, 300g)
- Herbs: parsley, rosemary, bay leaves

PREPARATION

1. Cut the vegetables and meat into small cubes.

2. Heat the olive oil in a casserole dish with a high flame, add the meat and brown well, then add the vegetables and chopped herbs. Stir for a couple of minutes, then add the white wine. Keep the flame high until the wine evaporates.

3. Add the salt and mix for a couple of minutes. The vegetables should start releasing all their juice. Reduce the flame to a minimum and cook for 2 hours, stirring occasionally to make sure nothing sticks to the casserole dish.

4. When the liquid is very reduced, tip the lot into a blender and blitz everything into a homogeneous paste.

5. To turn this gloop into a dry paste, spread it evenly onto an oven tray and bake it at 100°C for approx. 1 hour. Then turn off the oven and leave the tray in while it cools down. Flip the paste and repeat the whole drying process.

6. Now you have a dry paste you can crush and save into a plastic pot or a zip-top bag, ready to take to camp with you. This stock will last 2 months in the fridge, a couple of weeks out.

Blueberry Cornmeal Pancakes

Nowadays pancakes, especially blueberry have come to be seen almost as an American folk dish, but the basic recipe is ancient in origin, and packs a wholesome, filling, tasty punch.

INGREDIENTS

- 3/4 cup cornmeal
- 3/4 cup whole wheat flour
- 1/2 cup dried blueberries
- 1/2 cup raw wheat germ
- 1/2 cup milk powder
- 2 tsp baking powder
- 1/2 tsp salt
- 1 1/2 cups water
- Maple syrup
- Fresh berries (optional)
- Extra-virgin olive oil

AT HOME

Fill half of a zip-top bag with all the dry ingredients, shake and seal well.

AT THE CAMP

1. Add 1 1/2 cups of water to ingredients in the zip-top bag. Seal well and gently mix dry ingredients with water by massaging contents.

2. Heat up a skillet with a tbsp of olive oil. Scoop the batter out of the bag with a spoon into the hot skillet.

3. Wait until the batter begins to gently bubble, then flip. Cook till golden brown and repeat until you run out of batter. Add more oil to the skillet as necessary to prevent pancakes from sticking.

4. Build an impressive stack and drizzle the lot with maple syrup, fresh berries or banana spread (p. 77).

5. On the off chance you have leftovers pack them up – they're great as a snack.

Breakfast Porridge

Porridge is a healthy and hearty way to start a day in the wild. You can prepare it at home and save it in a zip-top bag, ready to cook at camp. Porridge has as many variations as its fans, this is our favourite camping combination.

INGREDIENTS

- 1 cup rolled oats
- 2 tbsp powdered milk
- 2 tbsp chopped almonds
- 2 tbsp dry fruit (cranberries, blueberries, dates, raisins)
- 1 tbsp sugar
- 1 pinch salt
- Spices: cinnamon, vanilla
- 2 cups water
- 2 tbsp honey (or maple syrup)

AT HOME

Put all the dry ingredients in a zip-top bag. Shake well to mix evenly.

Oatmeal cooks faster if cut in small pieces. If your rolled oats are whole grains, put 3/4 of them into a blender and roughly blitz them. Leave a few whole grains to keep the texture.

AT THE CAMP

Bring the water to a simmer then sprinkle in the oatmeal mixture while whisking. Carry on whisking until the mixture returns to the boil, then reduce the heat and cook at low flame for 5 minutes (the cooking time may vary depending on the type and texture of your oats).

Serve in bowls and top with honey or maple syrup.

Homemade Granola Bar

This energy bar is full of nuts, dried fruit and honey, and will recharge you when you need it most. What a great excuse to prepare such a deliciousness!

INGREDIENTS

- 2/3 cup quick-cooking oats
- 1/2 cup oat flour (or normal oats finely ground in a blender)
- 2 cups dried fruits and nuts.
- 1/4 cup sugar
- 1/3 cup honey
- 1/3 cup peanut butter
- 6 tbsp melted butter
- 1 tbsp cinnamon
- 1 tbsp vanilla extract
- 1/2 tsp salt

PREPARATION

1. Preheat the oven to 180°C. Line a pan with parchment paper and lightly grease it.

2. Smash the dried fruit and nuts in chunks, and mix them with all the other dry ingredients.

3. In a separate bowl, whisk together the melted butter, honey and peanut butter.

4. Toss the wet ingredients with the dry until the mixture is evenly crumbly. Spread evenly in the prepared pan.

5. Bake for 30 to 40 minutes until it's golden brown around the edges. Remove from the oven, allow to cool down, then rest in the fridge for a couple of hours (which binds all the ingredients together).

6. Cut the bars with a long knife and wrap them individually to store. They will keep well for a few days out of the fridge.

3
Recipes

You don't go camping to spend your day cooking. So our recipes are all about practicality, do-ability and above all, not wasting time. But that doesn't mean compromising on eating pleasure. With all the basic ingredients and pre-preparation tips we've given you so far, your trip really will have the best of both worlds.

All the recipes in this book are designed for 2 people with hearty appetites and a love of good food. If there are more than two of you, or you're really, really hungry, the recipes are very simple, so they're easy to scale up. But leave room for the delicious desserts you'll find at the end of this section.

Chickpea Flour Tortilla

This recipe is inspired by Italian 'farinata', but we've adapted it to our camping needs. In this version we've used mushrooms- better for fast cooking – but you can top your tortillas with any vegetable available. The thinner you cut most veggies – sliced courgettes or chopped asparagus and leeks – the faster they'll cook.

INGREDIENTS

- 3/4 cup chickpea flour
- 3/4 cup water
- 2 tbsp pre-made soffritto (p. 25)
- 4 big champignon mushrooms
- 2 tbsp extra-virgin olive oil
- Salt to taste
- Spices: ground pepper, rosemary, herbs to taste

TOOLS

- 1 stove
- 1 pan
- 1 bowl
- Knife and chopping board
- 1 long-handled spoon

PREPARATION

1. In a bowl mix together the chickpea flour and salt (if you have herbs, add them now). Slowly add a bit of the water, whisking all the time, until you get a smooth paste (NO lumps!).

2. Slowly add the rest of the water and keep whisking till you get a watery batter. Rest for at least 10 min to fully hydrate the chickpea flour.

3. While the batter is resting, finely chop the mushrooms. Then fry the soffritto in a skillet, in the olive oil, then add the mushrooms.

4. Cook the mushrooms for a couple of minutes, then add the batter and cover the skillet with a lid. Cook on a low flame, taking a peek every now and then, until the liquid is almost dry. Then flip the tortilla and continue cooking it until the pancake is cooked on both sides.

5. Turn onto a plate, season well, and serve while hot.

Tip: Make sure the pan is well oiled, or the tortilla can stick to the bottom. To flip the tortilla, cover the pan with a plate, then quickly turn both together to invert the tortilla onto the plate, cooked side up. You'll probably need to add a fresh glug of olive oil to the pan, and heat it up again. Then slip the inverted tortilla from the plate back into the pan, uncooked side down.

Tuna Pasta

This dish delivers maximum flavour, and yet it's almost bafflingly easy to throw together, and it delivers on pretty much every nutritional requirement. If you don't scoff the lot (unlikely), it makes a handy snack for when you're off on the next day's adventures.

INGREDIENTS

- 3 cups short pasta
- 2 cloves garlic
- 4 chunks preserved tuna
  (p. 29. Alternatively 1 can of
  shop-bought tuna)
- 1/3 cup white wine (optional)
- 1/2 cup sundried tomato
- 2 tbsp capers
- 10 green olives
- 2 tbsp walnuts
- 1 tbsp salt
- Spices: ground pepper,
  rosemary, parsley
- 3 tbsp extra-virgin olive oil

TOOLS

- 1 stove
- 1 pot
- 1 pan
- Knife and chopping board
- 1 long-handled spoon

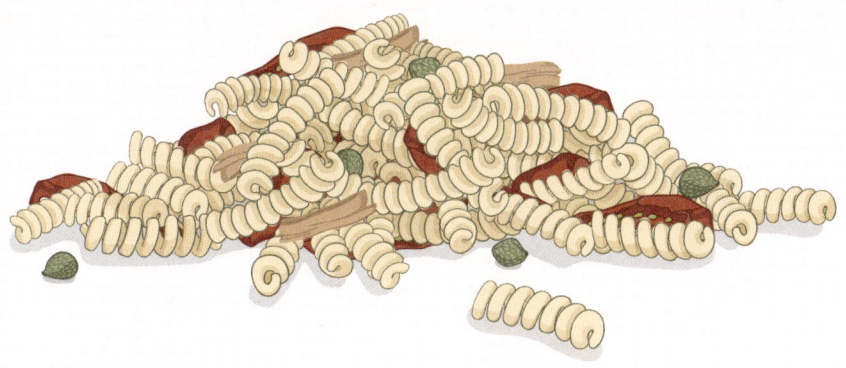

PREPARATION

1. Chop garlic, sundried tomato, green olives, parsley and walnuts in small pieces.

2. Fry the garlic in olive oil at low heat until golden brown.

3. Add the rinsed preserved tuna, sundried tomatoes, capers, olives and spices. Fry at high flame for 1 min and mix gently to toast the surface of the tuna. Don't mix too much, the final result must be chunky, not even.

4. If you have white wine, add it now and cook at high flame until you get a wet but not liquid mixture. Otherwise, use water. Once the sauce is ready, reserve.

5. Bring a pot of water to the boil, add the pasta and when it boils again, add salt and cook at medium heat as long as required for your pasta.

6. When the pasta is al dente, drain the water and add the tuna sauce, parsley and walnuts. Sauté the pasta with the sauce in the pot for 1 minute, and mix it gently so the pasta absorbs the sauce. You can add a little bit of olive oil to make it shine. Serve hot.

Veggie Couscous

Deliciously easy, couscous is always a favourite on our trips. It takes almost no time to cook, it goes with pretty much anything, and it fills your belly like few other meals. The best thing about this recipe is that you can mix it up with any vegetables you want. Just make sure they're all cut to similar sizes so they all cook evenly. Here is our coolest couscous meal.

INGREDIENTS

- 1 tbsp preserved soffritto (p. 25)
- 2 tbsp extra-virgin olive oil
- 1/2 leek
- 1 courgette
- 1 1/2 cup mushrooms
- 1/2 can chickpeas
- 1 cup couscous
- 1 cup water
- 1 tsp homemade stock (optional)
- Salt to taste
- Spices: ground pepper, curry powder...

TOOLS

- 1 stove
- 1 pot
- Knife and chopping board
- 1 can opener
- 1 spoon

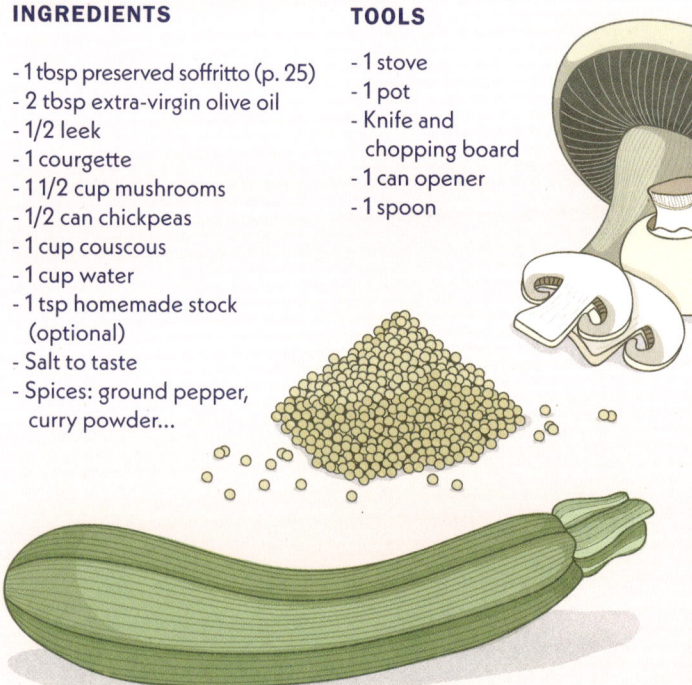

PREPARATION

1. Chop all the vegetables in small cubes.

2. In a big pot, sauté the soffritto in 2 tbsp of olive oil until translucent.

3. Add the chopped leek and cook them for one min.

4. Add all the other chopped vegetables, and the liquid from the can of chickpeas.

5. Add the cup of water, and the stock if you have it, then the spices, then bring everything to the boil.

6. Once the water is boiling, turn off the flame, then add the couscous. Mix and let it hydrate for 2 minutes.

7. The couscous is ready. Check the seasoning. You can add salt or soy sauce to enhance the flavour before eating.

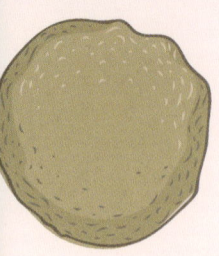

Quinoa Balls

Quinoa is a gluten-free grain, containing heaps of terribly important nutrients and is considered a superfood. Even better, it's delicious and quick and easy to cook, making it a perfect base for a spectacular camping meal.

INGREDIENTS

- 2 tbsp preserved soffritto (p.25)
- 1/2 cup quinoa
- 1 cup water
- 1 can chickpeas
- 1 bag breadcrumbs (p.26)
- Spices: parsley, curry powder...
- 4 tbsp extra-virgin olive oil
- Salt to taste

TOOLS

- 1 stove
- 1 bowl
- 1 can opener
- 2 pots
- 1 long-handled spoon

PREPARATION

1. Quinoa grains have something called saponins in their skins, which can have a too bitter taste. To get rid of them rinse the grains a couple of times in a bowl, with plenty of water.

2. In a big pot, sauté the soffritto in 2 tbsp of olive oil until translucent.

3. Add the rinsed quinoa, sauté for 2 minutes, then add the cup of water. Salt lightly and boil till the quinoa sprouts open up and the water is completely absorbed.

4. While the quinoa is boiling, open the can of chickpeas and use the can's lid to drain them. Then rinse them through once, still in the can, with clean water. Smash the chickpeas with a fork till you get a solid homogeneous paste. Add salt to taste.

5. When the quinoa is ready put it in a bowl and mix it with the smashed chickpeas and the spices. Mix until you get a solid, dry, homogeneous paste.

6. Make the mix into balls with your hands. Put the balls one by one into the bag of breadcrumbs, shake gently until each ball is completely bread-crumbed.

7. Heat 2 tbsp of oil in a pot, add a few quinoa balls, seal them on each side till brownish. Lower the flame and close the lid to create an oven effect. Bake the balls for a couple of minutes and serve them.

Stuffed Mushrooms

Fast, spectacular looking and delicious, this recipe will impress your camping mates. The secret is to fully rehydrate the textured soy with an aromatic smoked paprika juice to absorb its flavour. You can substitute the textured soy with minced meat if you have it.

INGREDIENTS

- 8 portobello mushrooms
- 2 cloves garlic
- 1 tbsp smoked paprika
- 1/2 cup textured soy
- 1/4 cup white wine
  (alternatively use water)
- 8 tsp grated cheese
- 3 tbsp olive oil
- Salt to taste

TOOLS

- 1 stove
- 1 large pot with lid
- Knife and chopping board
- 1 long-handled spoon

PREPARATION

1. Finely cut the garlic. Remove the stems from the mushrooms and cut the stems in small pieces.

2. In a large pot fry the garlic in the olive oil till golden brown. Add a generous amount of smoked paprika and cook while mixing for 30 seconds (not more or it will burn). Add the mushroom stems, keep mixing and cook for 2 minutes. Add the textured soy and stir well for a minute to absorb all the flavor. Add some wine (or water) to hydrate the soy, stir and cook until the liquid evaporates and you get a red grainy stuffing.

3. To fill the mushrooms, first add a pinch of salt (to release the juice of the mushrooms), then fill up with the stuffing. Top with a tsp of grated cheese.

4. Grease the same pot you've used for the stuffing with olive oil. Put the mushrooms in the pot (with the stuffed part on top) and cook with the lid on for 5 minutes at low flame. Serve.

Pizza, yes, Pizza!

Who says you can't enjoy a homemade pizza while camping?
This all-time favourite can be easily prepared using only one pan.

Top your dough with whatever you like – we've used cheese
and courgette, but you can use any vegetables, as long as they're
chopped into small, fast-to-cook pieces.

Our other favourite toppings are fresh tomato and raw rocket,
or mushrooms. Or try focaccia style, with olive oil, salt, oregano,
sundried tomato and capers, it's perfect accompanied by some dips.

INGREDIENTS

For the dough:

- 2 cups high-grade flour
- 3/4 cup water
- 1/2 tsp dry yeast
- 1 tsp salt

For the topping:

- Cheese to taste
- 1 small courgette
- Dressing: olive oil, oregano

TOOLS

- 1 stove
- 1 pan with a lid
- Knife and chopping board
- Grater
- Rolling pin
- 1 big bowl

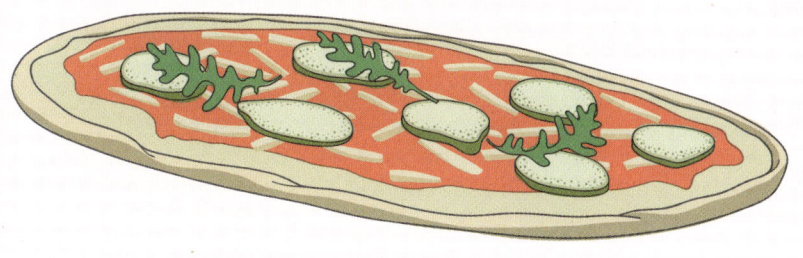

PREPARATION

1. In a bowl, mix together flour, salt and yeast. Add the water and knead till the dough is smooth (5 min). No worries if it's a bit sticky at the beginning, it will be fine once all the water is absorbed. After kneading, cover the bowl with a lid or a cloth and let the dough rise for 1 hour. Enough time for a nice walk, breathe in the fresh air and enjoy the view.

2. After the dough has rested, divide it into 4 smaller balls and rest them for another 5 minutes.

3. Meanwhile, grate the cheese and the courgette for the topping.

4. Roll out the dough into 4 circles 2 mm high.

5. Lightly oil the skillet and 'roast' the pizza for 1 minute on one side. Then flip it, add the topping then close the lid. Cook for a couple of minutes until the cheese starts melting.

6. Dress with olive oil and oregano and serve hot.

Lentil Burger

You might be out in the wild, but that doesn't mean you have to live like a caveman. This fantastic vegetarian burger recipe will satisfy even the most committed carnivore.

INGREDIENTS

- 1 can pre-cooked lentils
- 1/3 cup walnuts
- 1/2 onion
- 3 garlic cloves
- 2 tbsp breadcrumbs
- 2 tbsp extra-virgin olive oil
- 4 bread buns
- 1 tomato
- 4 slices Cheddar cheese
- Mustard to taste
- Salt, herbs and ground pepper to taste

TOOLS

- 1 stove
- 1 pan
- Knife and chopping board
- 1 zip-top bag

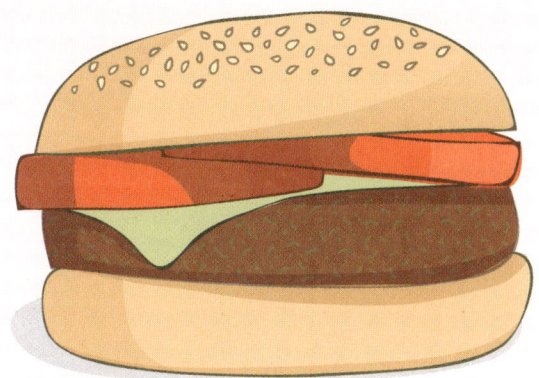

PREPARATION

1. Finely cut garlic and onion, smash the walnuts, rinse the lentils well and put everything into a zip-top bag together with the breadcrumbs, salt, pepper and herbs.

2. Squeeze excess air from the bag and smash the mix, massaging it with your hands until you get a uniform dense paste. Add more breadcrumbs if the mix is not dense enough.

3. Shape and flatten into four equally sized round patties about 1.5 cms thick, and let them rest for a couple of minutes.

4. Meanwhile you can prepare the toppings. Cut the tomato in slices. Open the buns and spread some mustard on the base.

5. Heat some olive oil in a pan and sauté the patties till they get a golden crust on both sides.

6. Assemble the burger in layers with the slices of cheese and tomato, add your favourite sauce, and enjoy.

Tip: To get a layer of melted cheese, towards the end of sautéing, slip a slice of Cheddar on top of each patty, then put the lid on the pan for a few seconds before serving up.

Mushroom Risotto

Rice isn't naturally a fast-cooking ingredient, but this doesn't mean you can't enjoy a good risotto while camping. There are heaps of brands on the market, with quick cooking times anywhere between 3 to 15 minutes. Pick the one that best fits your plans, remembering that rice with a longer cooking time will give you a creamier result. Dry mushrooms are long lasting, take up little room, and are virtually weightless – perfect for camping – but most importantly, they make delicious stock.

INGREDIENTS

- 1 cup dry porcini mushrooms
- 1 cup chopped fresh mushrooms (optional)
- 1 cup fast-cooking rice
- 2 tbsp preserved soffritto (p. 25)
- 4 tbsp extra-virgin olive oil
- 2 tbsp grated Parmesan cheese
- Salt and parsley to taste
- Soy sauce (optional)

TOOLS:

- 1 stove
- 2 pots
- 1 long-handled spoon

PREPARATION

1. Fill your bigger pot with warm water and soak the dehydrated mushrooms for 15 minutes.

2. Remove the mushrooms and keep them to one side. Bring the infused water to a boil, season with salt, then set it aside.

3. Sauté the pre-made soffritto in 2 tbsp of olive oil on a low flame until it gets brownish.

4. Add the hydrated mushrooms (and if you've got any, fresh mushrooms cut in cubes). Stir-fry for 2 min.

5. Add the rice. Stir-fry for 2 min.

6. Add some of the mushroom-infused water until the rice is covered and keep stirring the rice. When the water evaporates, add more to be sure the rice is always covered in water. Keep stirring. Repeat until the rice is cooked.

7. Add 1 more tbsp of olive oil and sprinkle with Parmesan cheese, parsley and a bit of soy sauce to supercharge the flavour.

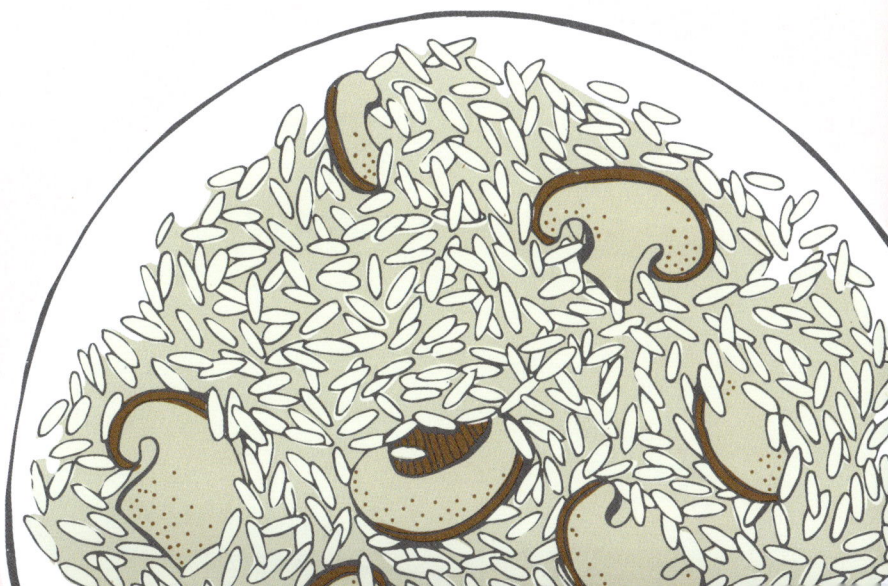

Beer Cheese Fondue

A fondue is a fun and social meal, and in good company, it's the ideal way to warm up a camping night. The inclusion of beer only adds to its magic. The addition of even more beer, drunk from cans or bottles whilst enjoying the fondue, further enhances this recipe's remarkable properties. It's easy to prepare and is the perfect excuse to join around a warm shared dish.

INGREDIENTS

- 1 clove garlic
- 1 can beer
- 1 cup grated Cheddar
- 1 cup grated Swiss cheese
- 1 tbsp cornstarch
- 1 tbsp mustard
- Salt, pepper, herbs to taste
- Dippers: broccoli, small potatoes, carrots, endives, chunks of bread...

TOOLS

- 1 stove
- 1 pot
- Knife and chopping board
- 1 long-handled spoon
- Forks

PREPARATION

1. First prepare your dippers. Blanch vegetables in chunks and set them aside for serving.

2. In a bowl, mix the grated cheeses with the cornstarch, pepper and herbs.

3. Rub the cut sides of a garlic clove around bottom and sides of a fondue pot.

4. Pour beer and mustard into the pot , stir and slowly bring to a simmer.

5. Gradually add the cheese mixture into the beer, keep stirring until the cheese is completely melted.

6. Season with salt and herbs and serve immediately. If the mixture gets too thick, rewarm it on a low to medium heat.

Tip: Your camping stove, if stable enough, is the perfect support to hold your fondue pot and keep it warm at low flame while eating.

Vegetarian Quesadillas

This Mexican-inspired recipe is super versatile, and you can make a meaty version by substituting textured soy with mince meat (preferably pork). If you're a neat eater, you might get away without using any plates, knives and forks.

INGREDIENTS

- 4 tortillas
- 1/2 cup textured soy
- 1/2 cup tomato puree
- 4 big slices Cheddar cheese
- 2 tbsp preserved soffritto (p. 25)
- 4 tbsp extra-virgin olive oil
- 3 tbsp canned corn
- 4 chopped champignon mushrooms
- 1 avocado, sliced
- Salt, pepper and powdered chilli to taste

TOOLS

- 1 stove
- 1 skillet
- 1 bowl
- Knife and chopping board
- 1 long-handled spoon

PREPARATION

1. Start with the soffritto. Heat the olive oil in a wide pan and add the homemade soffritto.

2. When the soffritto is golden brown, add the corn and the mushrooms. Check for seasoning (if you're using our preserved soffritto, you probably won't need to add any salt, but maybe some pepper and a dash of chilli powder to taste) and 'stir fry' for a couple of minutes.

3. When the vegetables are cooked, add the textured soy. Mix to moisten the textured soy with the olive oil, and cook for about a minute.

4. Add the tomato puree, cook for 5 minutes and pour off the sauce into a separate bowl.

5. Clean the same pan and dry it, then heat it up till it's VERY hot. Then add one tortilla and top it with a slice of cheese, then heat for 1 min until the cheese begins to melt. Cover half of the tortilla with some of the vegetably tomatoey sauce and a couple of slices of avocado, and fold the tortilla into a half-moon shape. When the quesadilla is fully toasted on one side, flip it and toast the other side. Serve and eat while hot.

French Toast

A classic recipe, ideal as a dessert or as an energy-laden breakfast.

INGREDIENTS

- 4 slices dry/old bread
- 1 cup long-life milk
- 3 tbsp sugar
- 1 tsp cornstarch
- Spices: vanilla, cinnamon, cardamom
- Extra-virgin olive oil

TOOLS

- 1 stove
- 1 pot
- 1 pan
- 1 long-handled spoon

PREPARATION

1. Warm up the milk (no boiling) and add 1 tbsp of sugar, cinnamon, vanilla, cardamom and cornstarch. Mix well.

2. Dip the slices of bread in the milk mix on both sides and reserve.

3. Heat up a pan with a bit of oil and fry the bread on both sides until toasted. Reserve.

4. Once all the slices of bread are cooked, clean the same pan and heat the rest of the sugar until it melts and gets a golden colour.

5. Add the slices of bread and caramelise both sides, be careful with this step because sugar can reach high temperatures.

Pan Tomaca Bread

Catalans use pan tomaca for almost everything. Great on its own, even better as a base for your sandwich or an accompaniment to your starters and/or mains. You can enhance it further with cheese, cured meat or whatever you like. Once you've tried this, you'll never look at bread in the same way again.

INGREDIENTS

- Bread: better if rye-based, or toasted
- 1 ripe tomato
- 1 clove garlic
- 3 tbsp extra-virgin olive oil
- Salt to taste
- Oregano (optional)

TOOLS

- Knife and chopping board
- Grater
- 1 spoon

PREPARATION

1. Cut the tomato in two and grate it into a small bowl.

2. Grate the garlic in the same bowl.

3. Season with oil and salt (and oregano if using) and mix well.

4. Spread a thin layer on your bread with a spoon.

Tuna Wrap

Easy, healthy, and super tasty. This rustic sandwich is ideal on extended excursions. Because it needs no cooking, you can bring the ingredients and prepare your sandwiches on the spot. (If you haven't prepared your preserved tuna at home, use canned tuna.)

INGREDIENTS

- 2 tortilla wraps
- 1 clove garlic
- Tuna in olive oil (p. 29)
- Salt, pepper, rosemary to taste
- 1/3 cup sundried tomato
- 2 tbsp capers
- 2 tbsp chopped olives
- 1 tbsp walnuts
- Extra-virgin olive oil

TOOLS

- 1 small bowl
- Knife and chopping board
- 1 spoon

PREPARATION

1. In a bowl mix together the rinsed preserved tuna (preferably homemade) with capers, smashed walnuts, chopped olives, thinly sliced garlic and sundried tomato. Season with a bit of extra-virgin olive oil, salt, pepper and rosemary.

2. Put the mixture onto a tortilla wrap, roll it up and voila! Your wrap is ready.

Aubergine Sandwich

An easy way to get a delicious, smokey, velvety, creamy spread from your eggplant/aubergine/whatever you call it, without using any pans or pots.

INGREDIENTS

- 2 pan buns prepapred with pan tomaca (p. 60)
- 1 small aubergine
- 4 tbsp extra-virgin olive oil
- 1 clove garlic
- 1/2 cup fresh mint leaves
- Salt and pepper to taste

TOOLS

- 1 stove
- Aluminium foil
- 1 fork
- 1 bowl

PREPARATION

1. Wrap the aubergine in aluminium foil and put it straight onto your stove (low flame!). Turn it a couple of times to cook it evenly. Stick the foil parcel with a fork, and if it enters easily, your aubergine is cooked.

2. Open the foil and peel the skin from the aubergine – it will come away easily and the inside should be soft and creamy.

3. Put the aubergine flesh in a bowl with the olive oil, salt, ground pepper, mint and finely chopped garlic. Mix together and fill your pan tomaca buns.

Dürüm Falafel

A truly international favourite, and tasty enough to please even the most fervent carnivore, this recipe could come from any Middle Eastern food truck, with the bonus of knowing exactly what's inside.

INGREDIENTS

For the falafel:

- 1 can chickpeas
- 1/2 onion
- 4 cloves garlic
- 3-4 tbsp chickpea flour
- 2 tbsp fresh parsley
- 2 tbsp fresh coriander
- 1 tsp salt
- 1 tsp baking powder
- 5 tbsp frying oil

For the garnish:

- 6 pita flat bread
- 1 tomato
- 1 onion
- Green salad
- 1/2 cup yoghurt
- 1 lemon
- 2 tbsp olive oil

TOOLS

- 1 stove
- 1 skillet
- 1 zip-top bag
- Knife and chopping board
- 1 long-handled spoon

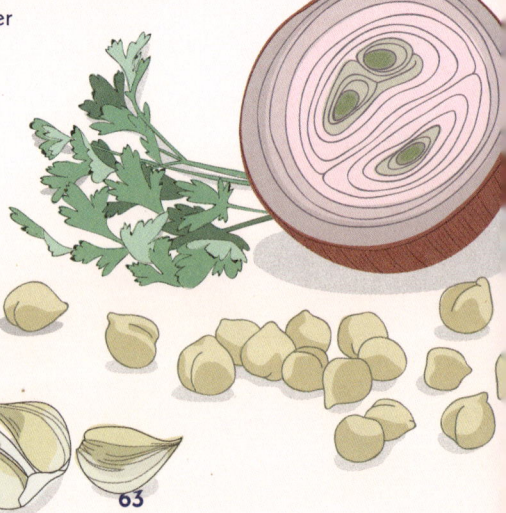

PREPARATION

1. Finely chop the onion, garlic, parsley and coriander. Thoroughly drain the can of chickpeas and put everything into a zip-top bag. Add the salt, chickpea flour and baking powder.

2. Mash and massage the contents until you get a moist even mixture that doesn't stick to the sides of the bag. If you want a drier mixture, add a bit more flour.

3. Form the mixture into 18 solid balls – these are your falafels. Put them to one side while you get on with the garnish.

4. Chop tomato and onion and cut the green salad into small pieces.

5. Prepare a yoghurt sauce by mixing yoghurt with the juice of 1 lemon and the olive oil. Season with salt and put to one side.

6. Heat a pan with plenty of frying oil and, when the oil is hot, fry the falafel balls on all sides till they are golden brown.

7. Place 3 falafel balls and some of the garnish in an open pita bread, fold the pita to form a roll, and repeat until they're all done.

8. Enjoy!

Veggie Paella

The secret of paella, and the one thing that makes it different from any other rice dish, is the 'socarrat', a thin layer of toasted rice at the bottom of the pan. This gives a unique taste and texture to the rice.

To get a perfect 'socarrat' you have to add the right amount of water to the rice and leave everything cooking until the rice is still moist, and yet almost but not quite dry. But, most important of all, once the rice goes in, NO mixing, ever. Never. Got that?

INGREDIENTS

- 2 cups short-grain rice
- 4 cups water
- 2 tbsp homemade stock (p. 31)
- 3 tbsp extra-virgin olive oil
- 2 tbsp preserved soffritto (p. 25)
- 1 med. to large sized tomato
- Mixed vegetables: green beans, artichokes, pepper, courgette, mushrooms...
- Salt, pepper, saffron, rosemary, and other herbs to taste

TOOLS

- 1 stove
- 1 wide flat-bottomed pan
- Grater
- Knife and chopping board
- 1 long-handled spoon

PREPARATION

1. Chop all your vegetables.

2. Put 3 tbsp of olive oil in a wide pan, add the soffritto (alternatively use 1/2 onion chopped), grate 1 tomato into the pan, and cook the lot for a couple of minutes until golden brown.

3. Add the vegetables, salt and herbs, and 'stir fry' on a high flame for a couple of minutes. When the veggies are lightly browned, add the water and the stock. Mix well and cook for 5 min.

4. Add the rice in an even layer, and cook on a high flame for 5 mins. Then lower the flame and simmer gently for 15 more mins *without mixing* until more dry than moist. If the rice is not perfectly cooked, you can add some more water (*still no mixing*), and cook until ready.

5. Turn off the flame, cover with a cloth, and let the paella rest for 5 more minutes before serving up and eating.

'Ota Ika Raw Fish

'Ota ika is a Polynesian dish, similar to Latin ceviche, made simply with raw fish marinated in citrus juice and coconut milk. Obviously, fresh fish can't last more than a day or even a few hours out of the fridge, so schedule this recipe towards the beginning of your meal plans. Nevertheless, this dish is ideal for a one-day excursion, or in case you're lucky enough to catch a fish while camping.

INGREDIENTS

- 1/2 k fresh white fish fillets
- 3 lemons
- 2 spring onions
- 1/2 cucumber
- 1 tomato
- 1/2 pepper (preferably green or yellow)
- 1 can coconut milk
- Salt and pepper to taste

TOOLS

- Knife and chopping board
- 1 big bowl
- 1 spoon

PREPARATION

1. Cut the fish fillets into small, bite-sized cubes, and put them in a bowl or a zip-top bag.

2. Squeeze the juice of the lemons onto the fish cubes, mix well and marinate for at least 1/2 hour in a cool place.

3. While you're waiting, slice the spring onions thinly and finely chop the tomato and the seeded pepper. Then peel the cucumber, cut it in half lengthwise and scrape out its seeds, then chop it finely.

4. After marinating, add all the chopped vegetables to the marinated fish, then shake up the can of coconut milk and pour it on the mix. Season with salt and pepper and mix well.

Tip: If someone wants a hot touch, serve some finely cut fresh chilli on the side.

Green Bean Fries

These 'no potato' fries are a healthy and easy-to-prepare camp snack. The chia seeds are a genuine superfood, and add to the fun- when wet, they turn into a sticky jelly which you use to coat the beans before breadcrumbing (instead of beaten egg yolks). You can breadcrumb almost anything with this easy method: aubergine, courgette, meat...

INGREDIENTS

- 1 cup green beans
- 1 tbsp chia seeds
- 4 tbsp water
- 1 breadcrumb bag (p. 26)
- 3 tbsp extra-virgin olive oil
- Salt to taste

TOOLS

- 1 stove
- 1 pan
- 2 bowls for mixing
  (or zip-top bags)
- 1 fork

69

PREPARATION

1. Start by hydrating the chia seeds with the water in a small bowl or a zip-top bag. Mix well and leave for ten minutes until they take on an even, jelly-like texture.

2. Meanwhile, chop off the ends of the green beans, and be ready with your zip-top bag of breadcrumb mix.

3. When the chia seeds are fully hydrated, mix them in with the green beans, making sure all the beans' surfaces are coated.

4. Now chuck the coated beans into your breadcrumb bag and shake them thoroughly so they're completely covered in breadcrumbs.

5. Heat the oil in a large pan, and when good and hot, fry the beans on both sides until the breadcrumbs are golden brown. You might want to do this in batches so that all the beans cook evenly. Season, and serve piping hot.

Skewers

There's an almost infinite number of possible combinations of things you can slide onto a skewer. Sweet or savoury, meat and/or veg and/or fruit, cooked or raw, any ingredients can be used as long as you consider a few important details: **1.** Combine a maximum of 4 ingredients: one as the main flavour, some to add contrasting flavours, textures or aromas, and some to add a touch of juiciness. **2.** If you're cooking your skewer on the bbq, stove top pan, or wood fire, use ingredients with similar cooking times. Here are some of our favourite combinations, each one accompanied by its perfect-fit dip.

CAPRESE

- Tomato (possibly cherry)
- Mozzarella cheese
- Basil

Sauce: Extra-virgin olive oil and Mediterranean herbs

KEBAB

- Lamb bites
- Aged cheese
- Pepper
- Onion

Sauce: Yoghurt, lemon juice, fresh mint

ANTIPASTO

- Melon
- Cured ham
- Rocket

Sauce: A few drops of balsamic vinegar will do

ENGLISH BREAKFAST

- Salmon
- Avocado
- Boiled egg

Sauce: Yoghurt, turmeric, dill, lemon juice, ground pepper

TROPICAL

- Sweet ham
- Pineapple
- Cheddar cheese

Sauce: A few drops of balsamic vinegar will do

SWEET DESSERT

- Strawberry
- Marshmallow
- Mint leaves.

Sauce: Hot melted chocolate

Sangria

There are many notions on how to best make sangria, but most of them are feeble approximations of the real thing. Authentic Spanish sangria is a subtly balanced melange of fruit flavours and wine, requiring time to infuse. So you need to plan your sangria at least 12 hours in advance, and be sure to have plenty of ice when you serve it. Yes, it requires a little effort but you will be completely rewarded if you follow this recipe to the letter.

INGREDIENTS

- 1 1/2 litres red wine
- 4 oranges
- 4 lemons
- 2 sticks cinnamon
- 4 tbsp sugar
- Loooots of ice

TOOLS

- Knife and chopping board
- A big jar (alternatively a big bowl)
- 1 long-handled spoon
- 1 strainer

PREPARATION

1. Pour the wine into a jar or a bowl. Squeeze the juice of two of the oranges and two lemons into the wine, then throw in the flesh and skin. Add the sugar and the crushed cinnamon sticks, and leave the mixture infusing at a cool temperature for at least 12 hours (if you have a fridge you can prepare it the night before, to serve your sangria the night after).

2. One hour before serving, sieve the liquid through the strainer, cut the rest of the lemons and oranges into slices or wedges, and add them to the infused wine. Leave resting for 1 more hour then add a lot of ice.

Tip:
Remove any fruit pips from the infusion, as they might release a bitter flavour.

74

Chocolate Ganache

After a day in the wild you deserve a treat. Prepare a spectacular, but healthy chocolate dessert with this easy recipe.

INGREDIENTS

- 1 cup dark chocolate (70% cacao) melted or broken in very small pieces
- 1/2 cup water
- 1 avocado (optional)
- 2 tbsp orange marmalade
- 3 digestive biscuits

TOOLS

- 1 stove
- 1 pot
- 2 glasses
- 1 long-handled spoon

PREPARATION

1. Bring the water to a boil, then add the chocolate.

2. Whisk well until you get a smooth, even mixture, then let it cool for at least 1 hour until it becomes firm. This is the ganache.

3. Assemble the glass in 3 layers: Put one tbsp of marmalade at the bottom, then add a layer of ganache in the middle, then top the lot with a crunchy layer of crumbled digestive biscuits.

Tip: If you can't cool your ganache, you can add one smashed avocado while the mixture is still hot and mix well. Your ganache will transform into a creamy mousse. Reserve at cool temperature.

Banana Crepes

Banana spread is a healthy, delicious accompaniment to crepes. Make enough and you can also use it as a homemade spread for toast, wraps and pancakes.

INGREDIENTS

For the batter:

- 3 eggs
- 1 cup high-grade flour
- 2 cups milk
- 2 tsp butter

For the banana spread:

- 3 fresh ripe bananas
- 1 lemon
- 1 tbsp sugar
- Spices: cinnamon, vanilla
- 1 tbsp rum (optional)

TOOLS

- 1 stove
- 1 bowl
- 1 frying pan
- 1 mixing bowl
- 1 whisking spoon
- 1 fork

PREPARATION

1. In a big bowl, whisk up the eggs, then add the milk, and mix thoroughly.

2. Slowly add the flour, keeping whisking to avoid any lumps, until you get a fluid, smooth, even batter. Put the bowl to one side.

3. While the batter rests for a few minutes, use a fork to mash the bananas in another bowl – you'll want a rough paste. Then drizzle them with the lemon juice, sugar and spices, then thoroughly mash them all together to finish off your spread. If you're going for it, now's the time to boost the bananas with a jigger of rum.

4. Heat a skillet and grease it lightly with butter. When the butter is melted pour in 1/4 cup of the crepe batter and gently swirl it around the pan so that it thinly covers the bottom of the pan. Cook for 1 minute on a low flame. Take a peek, and when the bottom side of the crepe is golden brown, flip it, and cook the other side for another minute or so. Put your crepe on a plate and repeat the process until you've used up all the batter.

5. To finish up your crepes, spread 1 tbsp of banana mixture on one side of each crepe, then roll them into tubes or fold them in half to make triangle shapes.

Cheese Cake

This is a truly idiot-proof recipe using ridiculously simple ingredients, and yet it delivers one of the most deliciously hedonistic, guilt inducing desserts imaginable. And on top of all that, it's packed with nutritious energy. Go figure!

INGREDIENTS

- 3 digestive biscuits
- 2 tbsp peanut butter
- 1 tsp sugar
- A pinch of salt
- 1/2 cup of cream cheese
- 1 tbsp of condensed milk
- A pinch of lemon zest
- 1 tbsp lemon juice
- 4 big chopped strawberries

TOOLS

- 1 zip-top bag
- 1 bowl
- 1 knife
- 1 spoon
- 2 jars (or cups)

PREPARATION

1. Put the digestive biscuits into a zip-top bag and smash them into small crumbs.

2. Add the peanut butter, sugar and salt and massage the bag to mix all the ingredients evenly.

3. In a bowl, mix together the cream cheese, condensed milk, lemon zest and juice until you get a smooth creamy texture.

4. Using a teaspoon, assemble the ingredients in layers into small jars (or cups): one layer of crackers mixture, one of cream cheese, and one of chopped strawberries.

Tip:
You can be creative with this recipe, so long as you keep a base of biscuits mixture and cream cheese. For instance, the cream cheese can be flavoured with vanilla or cinnamon. Substitute strawberries with other berries, or pretty much any sliced fruits. Another way of customising your cheese cake is to top everything off with a layer of muesli or banana spread (p. 77).

4.
Examples

Over the next few pages are some examples of how to plan and organise your meals for a range of camping options. Or go through our recipes and make your own plans – if you follow these guidelines you can't go wrong.

1. Figure out how many meals you'll need over the time you're away. Write them down as separate items throughout each day.

2. Make a list of all the ingredients you need for each of your meals. You'll use some food staples like olive oil, salt, and herbs across all of them, but you should still write them down.

3. Plan in some time for some home-preparing – it'll give you more free time while you're away.

4. Store all your ingredients in light but sturdy containers, preferably air or water tight. Pack them depending on your space and weight availability and think about the order you'll be using them up. Don't forget about refrigeration!

Road Trip

What better idea for a get-away-from-it-all week-end than heading off into the wild? Road trips are easy to improvise and cheap to pull off. Whether you're in a campervan or just throwing a tent in the car boot, you'll have plenty of space for a comfortable time away.

SHOPPING LIST

- Food staples: salt, sugar, herbs, garlic, smoked paprika, spices, extra-virgin olive oil...
- Bread
- Long-life milk
- Cornstarch
- Ground coffee
- Pasta
- Mushrooms (fresh and dry)
- Textured soy
- White wine
- Chickpea flour
- Fast-cooking rice
- Quinoa
- Canned chickpeas
- Nuts and dried fruit
- Fresh fruit (lemon and berries)
- Condensed milk
- Cheese (cream cheese, aged)
- Peanut butter
- Digestive biscuits

BASIC EQUIPMENT

- Gas stove and bottles
- Set of cooking pots
- Metal plates and cutlery
- Knife and chopping board
- Cups
- Big plastic bowl
- Zip-top bags
- Moka coffee machine
- Small glass jars for the cheese cake
- Paper towel roll
- Washing sponge and soap
- Chilly bin

HOME PREPARING

- Granola bar (p. 36)
- Soffritto (p. 25)
- Breadcrumb bag (p. 26)
- Sundried tomato pesto (p. 28)
- Porridge (p. 35)

THE MENU

For a weekend on the road you'll have: 2 breakfasts, 3 lunches, 2 dinners and some snacks for when you get the munchies.

BREAKFAST

Be sure you get enough energy before hitting the road.

- French toast (p. 59)
- Breakfast porridge (p. 35)
- Moka coffee (p. 17)

LUNCH

Aim for fast but energy-rich lunches. Less time cooking equals more time enjoying.

- Pasta with sundried tomato pesto (p. 28)
- Stuffed mushrooms (p. 47)
- Chickpea flour tortilla (p. 39)

DINNER

After a full day on the go you deserve a treat.

- Mushroom risotto (p. 53)
- Quinoa balls (p. 45)
- Cheese cake (p. 79)
- Sangria (p. 73)

SNACKS

Keep your energy levels high across the day.

- Granola bar (p. 36)
- Cheese cake (p. 79)
- Fruit and nuts

Kids Gone Wild

Picnics are a great idea, especially if you go with kids. A steady drip feed of treats is very important to keep everyone buzzing. Here are a few tips to have fun and get the right energy for an intense day outdoors (and a nice sleep that night).

SHOPPING LIST

- Food staples (salt, sugar, pepper, herbs, olive oil...)
- Lamb bites
- Cheese (mozzarella bites, cream cheese, aged cheese)
- Fresh veggies (cherry tomatoes, basil leaves, fresh mint, pepper, onion, courgette, green beans)
- Chia seeds
- Yoghurt
- Fresh fruit (lemon, strawberries)
- Digestive biscuits
- Peanut butter
- Condensed milk
- High-grade flour
- Dry yeast
- Nuts

BASIC EQUIPMENT

- Gas stove and bottles
- Set of cooking pots
- Metal plates and cutlery
- Cups
- Zip-top bags
- Knife and chopping board
- Coffee plunger
- Skewer sticks
- Paper towel roll
- Chilly bin

HOME PREPARING

- Hot chocolate bag *(p. 26)*
- Breadcrumb bag *(p. 26)*

THE MENU

For a 1-day picnic with the kids you'll need: 1 lunch, 1 dinner and lots of delicious but healthy snacks. Remember that our recipes are designed for 2 people, so scale up if needed.

LUNCH

It's a special day. The kids will love something colourful and fun, but that doesn't mean you can't give them healthy stuff.

- Skewers – Kebab & Caprese (p. 71)
- Cheese cake (p. 79)

DINNER

It's best to go easy on the sweet stuff at dinner if you want everyone to get to sleep at night.

- Pizza (p. 49)

SNACKS

Be sure you don't go short on fuel during the day.

- Hot chocolate
- Green bean fries (p. 69)
- Fruit and nuts

Hiking

Multi-day hiking is perhaps the best way of becoming one with nature, but being off the beaten track is one of the most challenging environments for cooking and enjoying decent meals. Each extra kilo in your backpack makes every step more of a trial, and you can't just 'pop back' for things you might have forgotten. So you must plan well, and keep to the essentials.

SHOPPING LIST

- Food staples (salt, sugar, pepper, herbs, garlic, curry powder, olive oil...)
- Maple syrup
- Fresh fruit
- Instant coffee
- Sliced bread
- Fresh tomato
- Capers
- Olives
- Pasta
- Dried porcini mushrooms
- Aubergines
- Fast cooking rice
- Nuts and dried fruit
- Tortilla wraps
- Quinoa
- Canned chickpeas
- Aged cheese

BASIC EQUIPMENT

- Gas stove and bottles
- Set of cooking pots
- Metal plates and cutlery
- Cups
- Zip-top bags
- Sealable airtight plastic pots
- Paper towel roll
- Aluminium foil
- Washing sponge and soap

HOME PREPARING

- Granola bar *(p. 36)*
- Soffritto *(p. 25)*
- Bag of pancake powder *(p. 33)*
- Sundried tomato pesto *(p. 28)*
- Bag of porridge *(p. 35)*
- Preserved tuna *(p. 29)*
- Hot chocolate powder *(p. 26)*

THE MENU

A 3-days hike should include: 2 breakfasts, 3 lunches, 2 dinners and plenty of snacks in between. Here is a selection of light, quick and easy-to-cook meals.

BREAKFAST

When you're spending your whole day walking, you definitely have to prime your energy pump with your first meal of the day. Together with some fruit, you could have:

- Cornmeal pancakes (p. 33)
- Breakfast porridge (p. 35)
- Instant coffee (p. 17)

LUNCH

While on your walk you probably won't have time to relax and create a comfortable space to prepare a proper lunch. So choose something very fast and easy to make.

- Tuna wrap (p. 61)
- Aubergine sandwich (p. 62)
- Pasta with sundried tomato pesto (p. 28)

DINNER

After a long day walking, you'll be tired, and you'll definitely deserve a nice hot energy-renewing reward.

- Mushroom Risotto (p. 53)
- Quinoa Balls (p. 45)

SNACKS

These are all perfect ways to boost your strength if you begin to flag.

- Granola bar (p. 36)
- Cornmeal pancakes (p. 23)
- Hot chocolate (p. 26)

Music Festival with Friends

When good friends, your favourite music and the great outdoors get together, good fun is guaranteed. Unfortunately, camp cooking for groups of people can be tricky, and you certainly don't want to be the one stuck behind the stove when the gig starts going off. These plan-in-advance preparations mean you get to enjoy great food without missing a beat of the festival.

SHOPPING LIST

- Food staples (salt, sugar, garlic, herbs, olive oil...)
- Spices: vanilla, cinnamon...
- Sliced bread
- Long-life milk
- Cornstarch
- Ground coffee
- Maple syrup
- Nuts and dried fruit
- Fresh fruit (berries, oranges, lemons)
- Couscous
- Fresh veggies (leeks, fresh mushrooms, courgettes, cherry tomatoes, broccoli, carrots)
- Pasta
- Cheese (Cheddar, Swiss)
- Beer and red wine

BASIC EQUIPMENT

- Gas stove and bottles
- Set of cooking pots
- Metal plates and cutlery
- Cups
- Zip-top bags
- Knife and chopping board
- Coffee plunger
- Skewers
- Paper towel roll
- Washing sponge and soap
- Chilly bin

HOME PREPARING

- Soffritto *(p. 25)*
- Bag of pancake powder *(p. 33)*
- Granola bar *(p. 36)*
- Pesto Genovese *(p. 27)*

THE MENU

A 2-day festival will consist of: 2 breakfasts, 2 lunches, 2 dinners and plenty of snacks for in between. Here is a selection of easy, fun, fast and sociable meals to share with friends.

BREAKFAST

You might need a boost of liquids, vitamins and sugar to head off any hangovers.

- French toast (p. 59)
- Cornmeal pancakes (p. 33)
- Plunger coffee (p. 17)

LUNCH

You'll be moving around more than you think so stock up on your carbs with these shareable meals.

- Vegetarian couscous (p. 43)
- Pasta with pesto
  Genovese (p. 27)

DINNER

Have dinner early, so you'll be set up for when the night gigs kick off. Sangria is an exotic option to spice up the night.

- Skewers (p. 71)
- Beer cheese fondue (p. 55)
- Sangria (p. 73)

SNACKS

Always bring some -you never know when you'll need a quick hit of extra energy.

- Granola bar (p. 36)
- Cornmeal pancakes (p. 33)
- Fruit and nuts

Beach Time

There's little truth in the old saying that you shouldn't swim after eating, but if you want to get back to the water quickly after lunch, you should keep things light and avoid fatty foods. This menu is high on simple, easy-to-digest energy sources, with a couple of treats thrown in. Most of it can be pre-prepared at home. Cooking on a beach can be a real pleasure (if you're shielded from wind), but always check with local regulations that it's OK to use a stove.

SHOPPING LIST

- Food staples: salt, sugar, herbs, rosemary, garlic, olive oil...
- Spices: cinnamon
- Fresh fish fillets
- Sliced bread
- Tomato
- Chickpea flour
- Mushrooms
- Red wine
- Fresh fruit: oranges, lemons
- Dark chocolate
- Avocado
- Orange marmalade
- Biscuits
- Ground coffee

BASIC EQUIPMENT

- Gas stove and bottles
- Set of cooking pots
- Metal plates and cutlery
- Cups
- Zip-top bags
- Knife and chopping board
- Coffee machine
- Skewer sticks
- Paper towel roll
- Chilly bin
- Windshield
- Washing sponge and soap

HOME PREPARING

- Preserved soffritto (p. 25)

THE MENU

For a day at the beach you'll need: 1 lunch, 1 dinner and some snacks.

LUNCH

If you catch a fish, brilliant, otherwise buy some on the way to the beach and pop it in your chilly bin.

- Ota ika *(p. 67)*
- Pan tomaca *(p. 60)*

DINNER

You can be back home for dinner but, are you going to miss the sunset?

- Chickpea flour tortilla *(p. 39)*
- Sangria *(p. 73)*

SNACKS

Be prepared for when the munchies arrive.

- Chocolate ganache *(p. 75)*
- Moka coffee *(p. 17)*

Leave No Trace

It's hard to put your finger on why camping is so appealing, just as it's hard to say why cooking more simply is so rewarding. And yet somehow, in abandoning 'civilisation', if only for a while, nature rewards us by resetting our perspectives on day-to-day life.

We hope you have enjoyed our camping cookbook and that it helps you make the very most of your adventures. In return, all we ask is that you leave the wild as you found it.

Index

Notes

Thank You!